LIGHT SPEAKS

Written by **Christine Layton**

Illustrated by **Luciana Navarro Powell**

TILBURY HOUSE PUBLISHERS

Awaking the world,
light speaks!

Light laughs in code,

signals in signs . . .

. . . and protects in patterns.

Light stretches far past sound.

Light tells the space between stars.

It echoes off planets and moons—

dappled,

glowing,

and brilliant.

From suns burned out

long ago,

still,

light whispers the answer to a mystery:

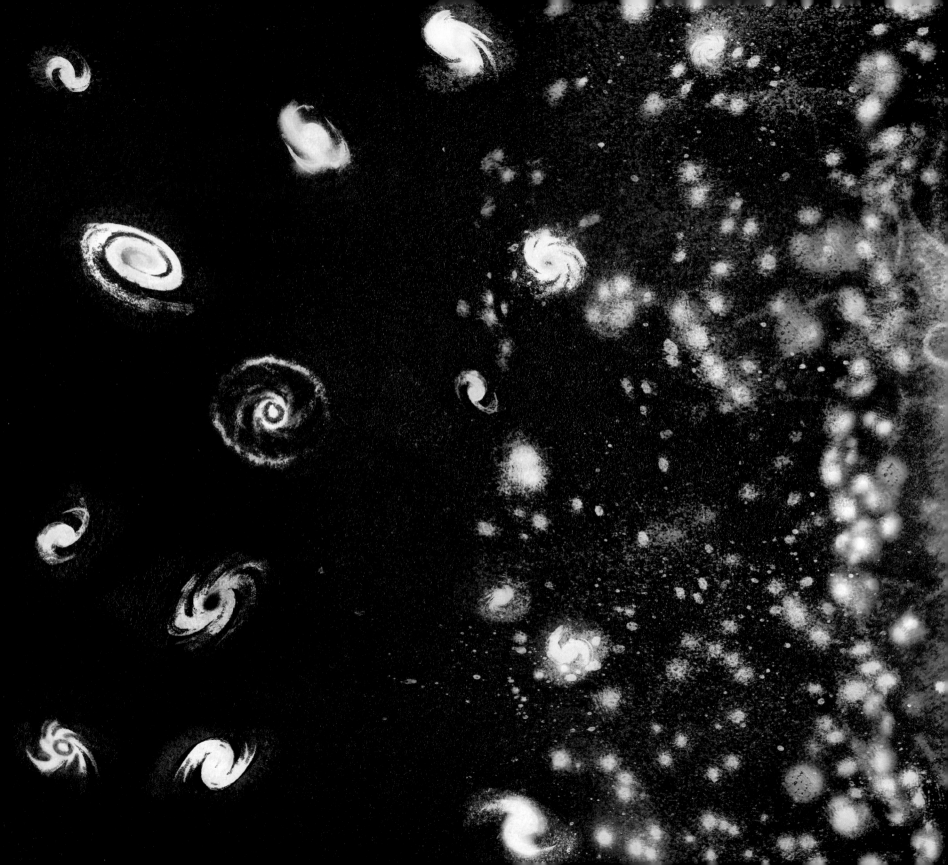

the start of time.

Light is a conversation from space to Earth

and Earth to space.

Once in a while, without meaning to, and without words,

light tells lies.

At times it looks angry
and sounds furious.

Sometimes light bursts and booms. Sometimes it burns, steady and quiet.

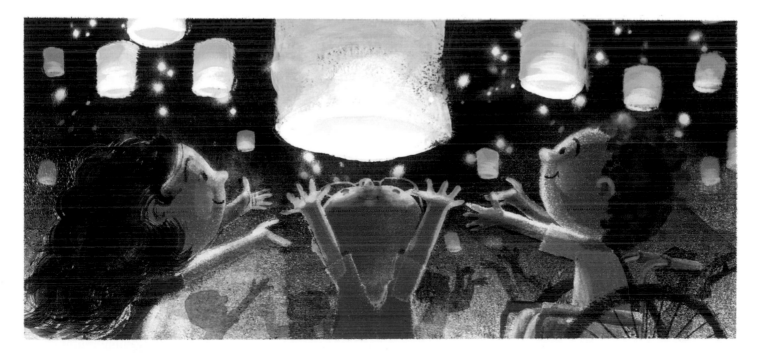

Lit pictures flip and dance like life.

Lit windows welcome
and warm the night.

And like a game, rays ask and answer,

"Are we the same?"

Light lets us see what's important.

Beaming, blazing, bursting,
flaming, flaring, glaring, glittering,

glimmering,

sparkling,

dazzling,

flowing,

glowing,

in moonrises, sunsets,

flashes, and streaks . . .

. . . light speaks.

More About Light

Light stretches far past sound

Sound waves travel through air in little pieces of matter called particles. Sound can't travel in space because there are no air particles there. Light waves don't need particles to move, so light waves can even travel through space. Light waves move about a million times faster than sound waves. If there is nothing blocking a light wave, it will keep moving forward in a straight line forever!

It echoes off planets and moons

Stars are burning balls of gas like our sun. Their fiery burn creates light. Planets and moons do not make their own light. We can see them in the night sky because light bounces off them. For example, we can only see Earth's moon when light from our sun bounces off it. When the Earth is in the way, blocking light waves from the sun, the moon is dark.

From suns burned out long ago, still, light whispers

Light waves travel 186,000 miles (300,000 kilometers) in a single second. At that speed, light waves take eight minutes to travel from the sun to Earth. The Butterfly Nebula in this illustration (as seen through the Hubble Space Telescope) is a glowing cloud of gas and dust formed by explosions of a dying star between the two "wings." That star may well be gone now, but we can't know that yet, because the light we're seeing started toward us 4,000 years ago.

...the answer to a mystery: the start of time.

The universe is expanding. Little by little, planets and stars move farther apart. Studying the distance between stars and how that distance changes over time, scientists can work backward to calculate how long it took the stars to arrive where they are now. Scientists can calculate all the way back to the Big Bang, when space and time were born together from an infinitely dense, infinitely hot kernel. By these calculations, our universe is about 13.8 billion years old. The illustration on these two pages shows the Big Bang at far right and the present day at far left.

Light is a conversation from space to Earth and Earth to space.

How far can astronomers see when they look into space? Light travels about 6 trillion miles (about 10 trillion kilometers) in one Earth year. This distance is called a light-year. The Hubble Space Telescope viewed a galaxy called GN-z11 that is 13.4 billion light-years away, and the James Webb Space Telescope is looking even farther. And what do astronauts see when they look at Earth from space? At night, from the International Space Station, about 200 miles (300 kilometers) above Earth's surface, astronauts see the artificial (human-made) lights of Earth's cities.

...light tells lies

Baby sea turtles hatch at night. To find the ocean, they look for bright moonlight reflecting off the water. However, to a baby sea turtle, the glow of city lights can look even brighter. Artificial lights can cause the turtle to crawl in the wrong direction, away from the ocean and into danger.

At times it looks angry and sounds furious

Thunderstorms occur when rising warm air's water droplets bump into cold air's ice crystals. The particles rub together, making static electricity. When the charge gets strong enough, energy zooms out from the cloud and then back up. It makes a flash of lightning and heat. The burst of heat spreads the surrounding air so quickly that the moving air makes a boom of thunder. Light waves have no sound, smell, taste, or feel on their own. These are all a product of reactions that can include light.

Light lets us see

Light allows us to see our world. You can see this book and the words on this page because light (from a light source) is bouncing off the paper. The paper does not create any light waves itself. What about color? Light from the sun contains all colors. When all of the light waves bounce off an object, we see white. When all of the light waves are absorbed into an object, we see black. The color of light that bounces off and goes into our eyes is the color we see. Red light waves bouncing off a rose make the flower look red to us.

Light Pollution

Many people know about water, air, and land pollution. Did you know there is also light pollution? Less than 100 years ago, we could see the Milky Way galaxy's countless stars in the night sky. Today, many people do not see stars at night from where they live. Artificial human-made light can cloud our view of the stars. It can also have a negative effect on our environment, especially for animals and plants that rely on the regular cycle of daylight and dark night.

    Fortunately, light pollution is reversible. To learn more, visit the International Dark-Sky Association at www.darksky.org/light-pollution/light-pollution-solutions.

Tilbury House Publishers
Thomaston, Maine • www.tilburyhouse.com

Text © 2022 by Christine Layton
Illustrations © 2022 by Luciana Navarro Powell

10 9 8 7 6 5 4 3 2 1

Library of Congress Control Number: 2022949609

Cover and interior designed by Frame25 Productions
Printed in China

*To my family, an
array of lights. —CL*

*To Michael, Alexander, and
Nicolas, my guiding lights. And
to the students and staff of
Assumption Catholic School
of Bellingham. —LNP*

Christine Layton has been a teacher for over thirteen years
and uses her early childhood literacy experience to create
engaging nonfiction curriculums for developing readers. Her
work has appeared in magazines, games, and assessments.
This is her first book.

Luciana Navarro Powell has created art since childhood. The colors, vibrancy, and warmth of her native Brazil infuse her work with
a sunny optimism, humor, and warm human-animal-landscape inter-
actions. As an immigrant, she wants all kids to be able to see them-
selves in her art. *Light Speaks* is her sixteenth children's book.